Just a Touch of Nearness

FRED BAUER

The C.R. Gibson Company,
Norwalk, Connecticut 06856

1

Just a Touch of Nearness

Just a touch of nearness—
    a smile, a wave, a word
Can miracle a leafless tree
    like a singing bird,
Just a touch of nearness—
    a hug, a kiss, a note
Can re-ignite an inner light
    and keep a soul afloat,
Just a touch of nearness
    is all it sometimes takes
To catch a lost and lonely heart
    before it falls and breaks.

ONE of my favorite teachers in college was forever telling students to take regular inventory of
their lives—to review their goals and to assess
how close they were to reaching them.

"Check your compass often," he advised, "and
make sure you're still on course. Life is too short
and time too precious to get waylaid by unproduc-
tive or unfulfilling ventures."

I thought about this wise man the other day while I was answering the letter of a young woman named Elizabeth from New England who had written me. She had read something I had said in a book on the subject of making a comeback after suffering a reversal ... that self-pity is counter-productive, that it drains us as if we were a bucket with a hole in it; that instead of promoting the healing process, self-sorrow extends it and exacerbates it.

"I don't seem to have any self confidence or belief in myself since my marriage fell apart," Elizabeth wrote. Her story was a familiar one: Pregnancy, followed by marriage, followed by tension and incompatability, followed by financial problems, separation and, finally, after more than six years, divorce.

"I should never have gotten married to him," she lamented, "and even after that mistake I should have cut my losses and gotten a divorce much sooner. If I had acted more promptly on the courage of my convictions, I might not now feel so demoralized and depressed."

What she did or didn't do yesterday, I told her, was not as important as what she does today. The most essential thing we need do after a setback—be it illness, death, divorce, loss of job or any defeat that causes us to lose self esteem—is to look forward, not backward. Following a reasonable "licking of our wounds" respite, we must take the initiative and reach out again to life and all its possibilities. There really isn't any other choice, and the sooner we embrace that conclusion the better.

Life is, after all, relationships. And in order to have good relationships, they must take place in close proximity with others. Keeping people at arm's distance may prevent the spread of germs, but it doesn't do much for love.

So Elizabeth, you must get on with the business of living and loving. You can't withdraw and become a hermit—not and be whole. Yes, you may get hurt again, but that is the price of admission to the most wonderful show ever conceived. Some disillusioned people try to live in isolation, hoping to spare themselves further suffering and pain, but that isn't living. It's only bare existence.

Circle the wagons, Elizabeth. Regroup and prepare to draw on your God-given inner resources. He endowed us with fantastic recuperative powers, and no matter how badly we've been treated, there are life-renewing waters deep within our souls. The Bible talks about that "still small voice" that prompts us all. If we listen closely, it will tell us where to go, what to do and when to do it.

❦

I'm reminded of a story that dates back to a time

when ice houses were common. One day the manager of an ice house in the Midwest lost his pocket watch among the huge crystal blocks. He and an assistant searched everywhere without success.

They were still looking, huffing and puffing and cussing, noisily moving the ice from one place to another when a young boy came by and asked what they were doing. When they told him, he said that he thought he could find it. The men were dubious, but they agreed to let him try.

Alone, the boy entered the ice house and closed the door. In less than a minute, he emerged with a big smile on his face and a gold watch dangling from a chain he held in his hand.

"How did you ever find it?" they wanted to know.

"I just got down on my knees, put my ear to the floor and listened," he said.

To get in touch with yourself, find a quiet place and take time to listen to what your soul is saying. And to get in touch with others, take the first step and reach out to them. Often others are just waiting for us to show some small flickering of interest. Salvation, for all of us, is through love—how we receive love and how we give love. And it all begins, I believe, with...just a touch of nearness.

2

You're Somebody Important

❦

Instead of mourning things you lack
and what is not,
Thank the Lord for what you are
and what you've got.

"WHAT a tragedy," everyone said, and of course it was. Jerry deserved sympathy. But I knew when I went to visit him that pity was not what the young man needed or wanted.

The accident had left his legs permanently paralyzed and doctors had told him he wouldn't walk again. Considering the fact that he had been an exceptional athlete and that his enthusiasm for life had seemed to know no bounds, it was a double blow.

After some pleasant preliminaries, I asked him about his plans. Like a cloud eclipsing the sun, his handsome face darkened and his eyes hardened. "I have no idea what I'm going to do," he hissed. "I hate the thought of getting up each morning."

I reminded him that he still had a good mind, 11

his eyes, his ears, his arms and hands, but that seemed little solace. What was left, he said, was not enough…his life was ruined. I left a few minutes later, a little shaken, not from Jerry's physical change, but from the metamorphosis of his attitude. The accident had totally transformed his personality.

Some time later I saw Jerry again, rolling toward me in a wheelchair. His sun-tanned face was radiant. For a minute I wasn't sure it was he—Jerry.

"Hello, there," he called brightly. In quick order, he told me he was back at work, handling sales orders over the phone; that he was coaching a baseball team, that he had taken a leadership role at church and that he was doing volunteer work.

"What's more I've met a fantastic girl…"

All this was wonderful news, but the most intriguing thing to me was how Jerry had turned things around. When I finally asked him about his 180-degree swing, he shared this with me:

"My physical therapist said that there are three kinds of people in the world: well poisoners, parade watchers and life enhancers. We each choose which kind we want to be. I made up my mind to be the latter. Now I don't have time to do everything I want to do. I can't wait to get started each day. I'm in love with life."

Poet E.E. Cummings may have said it best, for certain most simply: *Without love nothing else makes any sense.* In Jerry's case, his accident left him feeling half a person, and he didn't think in his lessened state he could love himself any more. And had he not gotten on top of those self-destructive feelings, he would have lived the rest of his life a beaten man.

There is one thing about self estimation of which I am absolutely certain: When we can't accept ourselves, don't feel self worth or believe we are unlovable, then we are incapable of loving someone else.

In addition to being a good friend to others, we need to be a good friend with ourself. But you and I are often guilty of thinly veiled self-hatred— much too demanding, much too critical and much too hard on ourselves. And thinking more poorly of ourselves than we ought can turn us into inert monuments of self doubt.

Somewhere along the way many of us may pick up the warped notion that we are less than lovable, less than worthwhile, less than capable, and as a result become emotionally handicapped. Instead of reaching out spontaneously when affectionate words or actions would be appropriate and appreciated, we abstain or withdraw, afraid of being misunderstood or sounding foolish. Eventually we seem to lose our ability to show sensitivity and kindness in situations that call for intuitive expressions of caring and concern.

❦

Where or when or why do people develop debilitatingly low opinions of themselves? For many individuals such negative feelings begin at a very early age. Parents, teachers, family members, friends and neighbors, church and community leaders obviously have a tremendous influence on how we view ourselves. If a child repeatedly hears that he or she is stupid, awkward, homely, unreliable or lazy, it won't take long before that child feels unworthy and inferior. Such destructive conditioning usually does one of two things: turns us into cynical clams who retreat into our shells, or caustic vipers who spit out venomous criticism.

Remember how self conscious we were of our appearance as adolescents? Looking in the mirror at our complexions, hair, noses, ears, teeth, muscles or figures was an obsession for most of us when we were teenagers. And if anyone ever made a derisive comment about our looks, we were wiped out for weeks.

I recall one day before a basketball game (I must have been in junior high school) overhearing a teammate tell another player, "At least I don't look as skinny in my uniform as Bauer." I think I sent off for the Charles Atlas body building workbook that very night. (Now if I could just keep that roll from creeping over my belt.)

Fortunately, for most of us, there comes a time when other things take precedence over how we look. But some of us only traded our old anxieties for new ones—our family backgrounds, the amount of our education, the size of our bank accounts, where we live, how big a house, and so on.

Once we believe that we have been short-changed by either the Lord or some other life force, it is hard to erase such imprints from our minds. We can easily justify our lack of production or performance by "the poor hand we've been dealt."

❦

The truth is that none of us are perfect packages. We all have some shortcomings and some hangups. Once I interviewed Tom Dempsey, the former professional football player, for a magazine article. Tom was born with a deformed right foot, which seemingly would have ended any thought of him being much of an athlete. But Tom had some very unusual parents who encouraged him to set his own limits, and as a result he joined the high school football team.

His forte was kicking. A special shoe was designed for him and he became outstanding at his specialty, so much so that he went on to play in college and, almost unbelievably, in the pro ranks. His most amazing achievement came one day when he kicked a 63-yard field goal, a record that still stands!

When others marvel over his accomplishments, Tom shrugs it off as nothing. "We all have handicaps," he told me, "the only difference is that some show, some don't."

There is one other difference: how we cope with our handicaps. Some people, like Tom Dempsey, refuse to let them control their lives. They come from the "mind over matter" school and won't give in or give up.

❧

We once owned a dog that possessed that kind of mettle. He was pure mutt, one of the homeliest dogs you've ever seen, but also one of the smartest. When Scampy got hit by a car and suffered a broken hind leg that became gangrenous, the vet said he should be put to sleep.

"He means *killed*!" one of my children screamed with tears running down his face. "Doctors don't kill people with bad legs."

A family council voted for amputation instead, and I agreed, though for several weeks I feared the decision might have contained more sentiment than soundness. Then, one day, I looked out my study window and saw Scampy, sunning in the yard. His focus was on a squirrel that had come through the fence.

Prior to his surgery, the only thing that seemed to give him more pleasure than running with me on morning jogs was chasing squirrels. Since the operation, he hadn't been accompanying me in the morning. Now if he couldn't even police the yard of squirrels, I thought, it would be strong evidence that his operation had been a mistake.

But slowly Scampy raised himself into the attack position, and then *boing*, as if propelled off a pogo stick, he shot up into the air and gave that squirrel the scare of his life. When Scampy returned to his sunning spot, he carried himself as proudly on three legs as he ever had on four. And from thereon his recovery was phenomenal.

Scampy is gone now, but the other day I recalled what someone observing his three-legged enthusiasm had once said: "The beautiful thing about Scampy is that he doesn't seem to know he's handicapped." And I'm convinced he didn't. The law of compensation in life is miraculous. The blind learn to see with their ears, the deaf to hear through touch.

What a blessing it would be for all of us, if we could put our shortcomings, real or perceived, out of our minds and concentrate on our assets instead. If each of us could, we wouldn't ever have to feel inferior again—or superior. Only equal.

I have good news for people who feel that they are life's leftovers or leftouts. You are special and distinctive. No one has quite the same makeup as you do, physically, mentally or spiritually. Your experiences give you a perspective unlike anyone else. You were placed on earth for a purpose and God gave you the talent for achieving it. The Bible tells us that we are created in God's image ... and that we are imbued with great potential, capable of more than we have ever dreamed, touched by divinity, created to demonstrate creativity. In the words of the great soul singer Ethel Waters, *"God don't make junk."*

But to achieve our unique purpose and to fulfill our destiny a change in operating procedure may be needed—we may have to alter our attitude and behavior. Instead of being passive collectors of love, we need to become reflectors of it, too. We need to become rivers of love, flooding others with our friendship,not reservoirs, damming the waters and staunching the flow.

What we must do, in the last analysis, is what Jerry did—cast our lot with the life enhancers, not the well poisoners or the parade watchers. And we must begin today.

3

The Healing Power of Touch

❦

It's not well-chosen words or their amount,
It isn't time or flowers or cards that count,
But rather that we come in hope of
Subtracting grief and adding love.

ONE of the special ministry's of the church-run hospital was to give help to unwed mothers. The doctors provided prenatal checkups, counseling, delivery and recovery care—often without charge. Because many of the women chose to put their babies up for adoption, the hospital's nursery was separated by some distance from the maternity ward, the thinking being that it would be less traumatic if the mothers giving up their children would not be able to hear them crying.

It was a well-run hospital with a friendly and dedicated staff. The health care was the finest available anywhere. That's why it was such a shock when the hospital's newborn mortality rate showed a sudden increase. Perfectly healthy babies had died without apparent cause. Medical examiners were called in to study the phenomenon. They reviewed each case trying to find some clue. Tests were conducted, procedures reviewed and then reviewed again. There was nothing to explain the mysterious rise in infant deaths.

Then one day, one of the examiners made an off-hand observation about the nursery personnel: "You seem to be short-handed on the third shift," he said.

The hospital administrator explained that an elderly woman, a nurse's aid, had retired and not been replaced. "Mother Dora was something of a fixture around here," the executive explained. "She loved babies and took care of them as if they were her own. No baby cried for long without being picked up and cuddled and sung to when Dora was on duty."

"And now?" asked the examiner.

"Well, the babies probably aren't held as much. Could it be...?"

The next day a notice went up on the nursery bulletin board: *Beginning today, all babies are to be held a minimum of 10 minutes each hour.*

And the problem went away.

❦

Once we thought food and sleep and warmth were about all that babies needed to be healthy. Now we know that they need to be held, too. And so do we all whether we are one day or 100 years old.

Touch, it seems, is an essential not only for establishing and maintaining our sense of well-being, but also for our healing and restoration when we become sick of mind or body. *Man does not live by bread alone...*

One of the most dramatic stories I've ever heard about the healing power of touch was told to me one time by an Ohio woman who had lost her eyesight. She was legally blind and doctors said she would never see again.

Then, one day her husband announced that he was going to take her to a healing service at a large church in a nearby city. "I believe the Lord can heal you," he said.

"I believe He can, too," she answered good naturedly, "but I don't believe He will until I get to Heaven." Nonetheless, almost as a favor to her loving husband, the woman accompanied him to the service and went forward when the minister invited all who needed healing to come.

"When the pastor inquired about my problem I told him, and he prayed for me. Then, he put his hands on my head and I felt a great surge of electricity and I saw a light brighter than the sun. I believe it was God touching me through the minister's hands...and suddenly for the first time in 15 years I could see."

"Perfectly?" I wanted to know.

"Not at first," she answered, "but eventually I could see well enough to sew and read again."

"What do you make of it?" I asked.

"The thing speaks for itself," she replied, and so it did.

I don't know what to make of this woman's experience then nor do I now. Little miracles like the birth of a baby or the annual March appearance of daffodils on the south side of the house, I can handle. Bigger miracles cause words to catch in my throat. The kind I described here raises as many questions as it answers. Though the woman whose sight was restored was a person of deep faith, I know that she didn't bombard God with prayers, petitioning Him to heal her. A warm and tranquil woman, she had come to terms with her blindness and seemed to accept it without much complaining. So the question, "Why her?" is a tough one to answer. The only observation that seems inarguable is that she was touched by the minister's hands which served as a healing conduit.

❧

Her experience and that of a woman in the New Testament have much in common, and both are thunderous testimonies to the healing power of touch.... One day Jesus was passing through a crowd which was pressing about him. Suddenly, Christ stopped and asked, "Who touched me?"

His disciples thought His question strange; thousands had brushed against Him. But this touch was different—not the casual touch of many, but the intended touch of one.

What we learn is that a very sick woman had struggled through the crowd, believing that if she could but touch His garment, she would be healed. The Gospel writers inform us that she had sought to be cured by doctors for 12 years, had spent everything she had trying to find a remedy, but had only gotten worse.

Summoned from out of the crowd, the ailing woman came forward and admitted, trembling, that yes, it was she who had touched the Master.

"Your faith has made you whole," Jesus told her, and she went away, healed.

❦

Reaching out to be touched…or reaching out to touch another are both faith acts of great significance because each serves to activate the healing current of love. There are many kinds of healing, and we have an opportunity to be God's agent for one or more of them every day. The discouraged and depressed need healing words of encouragement and approval. The lonely need our understanding hearts and attentive ears. The sick and suffering need our intercessory prayers and our willingness to help. And those who mourn need our undergirding closeness when hope is far away.

When it comes to comforting the bereaved, many of us are uncomfortable, fearful that our prosaic words are inadequate. It is good to remember that the most important thing we can bring is ourselves. Our very attempt to reach out and touch those who are hurting testifies to the love and concern in our hearts more than anything we say.

I once heard about the tragic traffic death of a young child. Nancy, just six years old, had been struck by a speeding car. Her parents were devastated. So were her schoolmates, especially Joyce, Nancy's closest friend. As soon as Joyce heard the news about Nancy, she wanted to run to her friend's house. But Joyce's mother thought it would be too upsetting for their daughter and for Nancy's parents. "Daddy and you and I will go to the funeral," she consoled. "You can see Nancy's parents there." But a tearful Joyce insisted that she must see them immediately.

What worried Joyce's mother most was what she herself might say to the grieving parents. But finally, reluctantly, she agreed to take her daughter to Nancy's house. And when they arrived, Joyce ran to her lost friend's mother, climbed upon her lap and threw her arms around her. Wordlessly, the two of them cried out their mutual hurt.

No one who came to say "I'm sorry," said it better than Joyce.

4

When It's Our Turn to Crank

&

True love is profligate,
it gives itself away,
Withholding naught a bloom
from its sweet bouquet.

THE slightly-built boy of eight lay on his bed clad only in his pajama bottoms. On the night-stand under a lamp was an opened math book, face down. His mother, sitting beside him, brushed stray wisps of dark hair from his fevered forehead and talked in soothing whispers.

"I called Doctor Williams and he said there is a lot of flu around. He suggested aspirins, liquids and plenty of rest. He said you would probably feel better in the morning."

"I hope so."

Then she opened a jar that she had brought from the bathroom. From it she drew an ointment that she dabbed first under his nose and then spread over his chest. The mentholated vapors filled the room with the promise of healing. But it was not the odor of the ointment or its smoothness that made him sigh with contentment, but the gentle, rhythmic motion of his mother's hand. He could still feel her comforting touch as he drifted off in sleep, long after she had kissed him good-night and left the darkened room.

❦

The memory of such chest rubs by my mother are some of the most vivid of my childhood. It almost makes me think I enjoyed being sick.

In truth what I enjoyed and what we all enjoy is the attention, the feeling that we are important to someone we love, that we are special. But those halcyon moments are too few and too fleeting. We grow up, and much before we're ready to give up the comforts of childhood, we are mantled with the heavy responsibilities of adulthood.

The fear of such a yoke was the sub-theme of a film I saw not long ago. It was about a man who was feeling the pressures of adulthood crowding in on him. He had just turned 40 and recently discovered his own mortality. (That's about the time many of us realize that we really aren't going to live forever.) His recently widowed mother, his divorced sister, his overly-dependent wife and his spoiled children all saw him as family patriarch, capable of addressing and resolving all their difficulties.

He complained bitterly that it was too soon in life for him to have to shoulder all this responsibility. One night in a dream he saw himself standing before a judge asking for relief. But the judge was not the least bit sympathetic.

"I sentence you for the rest of your life to be the Daddy."

"But I don't want to be the Daddy," the man screamed back. He was still screaming the line when he was awakened from the dream by his wife.

❧

Oh, to be able to hold onto the sweet comforts of childhood. To be cradled in youth's sweet arms all our lives. But like it or not, there comes a day when we must think less about being stroked ourselves and more about stroking others; when we must administer the mentholated ointment instead of receiving it.

One of the secrets of growing into this role gracefully is, I believe, the acceptance of life's unfolding drama as not only a natural phenomenon, but as a privileged one. Growing older and being asked to put something back into the pot we've been drawing from should neither surprise us nor fill us with resentment. It's time to get on with the next act. Raise the curtain!

❧

A couple of years ago I was more than a little apprehensive about becoming a grandfather. Much too young. But that was before I knew the sweetness of a granddaughter's hugs and kisses. Now I can't wait for the arrival of the next one.

Once I thought that people who were adept at nurturing others—helping them grow, making them feel special—had been divinely gifted. But I have come to believe that nurturing is an acquired skill. All anyone really needs to dispense such bounty is a modicum of selflessness. Most of us are capable of a little self-denial on occasion, though we are often inconsistent and fickle. Yet, with more practice, more concentration and commitment, I am convinced that almost anyone can get the hang of it. Old dogs can be taught new tricks when the rewards are so delicious.

I'd compare it to turning the crank on our mechanical ice-cream freezer. One of the joys of summer at our house is homemade ice cream. But my wife Shirley, who disdains electric freezers, insists that everyone—family and guests alike—must turn the crank or the quality of the product will suffer. What my Ohio-bred sweetheart knows but doesn't say is that cold ice cream tastes twice as good on a hot day if the eaters have worked up a sweat making it.

Every once in a while I meet saints who show me what real giving is all about, and, like the measles, what they are peddling is infectious. They show me what it means to *"love the Lord thy God with all your heart, soul, mind and strength, and your neighbor as yourself."*

Such people are a couple I know who tried to have children for several years without success. Finally, they turned to adoption agencies, but the only children available were ones with mental or physical handicaps. Nowhere could they find that perfect blond, blue-eyed baby of their dreams.

"Lord, help us find a child," the woman prayed without any results. Then, one day, God spoke to her heart. "I have showed you scores of children that need you, but you have rejected them because they are imperfect. You and your husband cannot have children because of your physical imperfections. Together, you and the children have mutual flaws and mutual needs. Reach out to these little ones and find the joy you seek."

So, with great trepidation, she and her husband adopted a little girl who had a congenital deformity. But the love they gave and the love they received in return soon blinded them to her handicap and to the handicaps of other "unadoptable" children. Over the years they have adopted and/or served as foster parents for more than a dozen children that no one else would take…

"Lord, when did we see thee hungry and feed thee, or thirsty and give thee drink? And when did we see thee a stranger and welcome thee, or naked and clothe thee? And when did we see thee sick or in prison and visit thee?" And the King shall answer them, "Truly, I say to you, as you did it to one of the least of these my brethren, you did it to me."

5

Words That Alienate, Words That Resuscitate

——— ❦ ———

*Friends are those who take us
unjudging by the hand,
Who, feigning blindness,
overlook and understand.*

THE news services handled the story as if it were a rarity, but aside from the timing involved, the details are all too common. Two brothers who had gotten into an argument 25 years before over the settlement of an estate had vowed not to meet or speak again, and for a quarter of a century they had kept their word.

But recently they were reunited...in a hospital. Their reunion was not, however, of their own doing. Though both were residents of the same city, they lived and worked in different sections, and they were on their respective jobs when events happened that brought them together. One brother was injured in an industrial accident, the other suffered a heart attack. Both were rushed to the same hospital's emergency room where doctors tried to save them. Medical efforts failed, and the brothers both died—in the same room, on the same day, only a short time apart. But they had kept their word; they never spoke to each other again.

❧

The sad thing is that their relationship could have been different. I know that without knowing the particulars. If only one or the other had picked up the phone some Saturday morning and said, "Charley, I've been thinking about our situation and I'm sorry." Or if one had sat down and written a short note that said, "I was wrong and want you to know how much I miss seeing you."

Unfortunately, neither took the first step, and the breach went unmended. What the brothers needed to do and what we need to do when words separate is to find words that rejoin. But we avoid saying them in the same way that we avoid poison ivy. Because our pride is involved and nothing keeps wounds from healing like pride. And nowhere is this more evident than in strained or broken family relationships.

Why is it that there is so much hostility among family members? So much bitterness and alienation? Does it have to be, as they say, that we often hurt those we love? Why can't we learn to disagree without being disagreeable? More to the point, do we have to remain at odds after an argument or clash has run its course? Not unless we are masochists or sadists.

No story anywhere better illustrates the joy of forgiveness and reconciliation than Christ's parable of the Prodigal Son, and no scene in the Bible tugs as hard at my heartstrings...

To begin with, the Dad in the Bible story shows great understanding of human nature when he allows his son to leave the farm and pursue his dream. The father loved his son enough to let him go, to let him fail, if necessary. But the part of the story that brings a tear to my eyes every time I hear it is when the father sees his son returning.

If you've ever lived on the farm, you know the daily ritual of going out front to the mailbox. In my mind's eye, I see Dad standing by a mailbox, looking through the mail. When he finishes sorting through the envelopes, he shakes his head and looks at the ground. No message from his son... still.

Discouraged, he is about to return to the house where he will tell his wife again, "No word from Joe." But before he leaves the roadside, he looks up the pathway to where it rises to meet the sky. He has searched that same heat-distorted horizon for months, hoping that he might catch sight of his son. He had this feeling...

34   But when Dad looked today, he saw a figure

coming toward the farm, and his heart beat faster. At first he wasn't sure it was his son, the figure was so thin and so bent over. But there was something about his gait, the tilt of his head, the way his corn-silk hair danced in the wind, that gave Joe away.

And so the father started running toward that lonely figure. He couldn't wait to embrace him. He didn't hesitate for a second, didn't hang back. Nor did he wait for the boy to come to him, to prostrate himself, to pour out his regrets, to beg forgiveness. No, the father just ran to him and threw himself tearfully into the boy's arms.

❦

End of story? All lived happily ever after? No, Christ didn't deal in fairy tales, but real life. And just as it often is in life, not everybody was elated over the prodigal's return. His older brother was really bent out of shape when he observed the fuss being made over Joe. All the robes and rings and fatted-calves business made him want to scream.

"Hold on there, Dad," I can hear him complaining. "I've been breaking my back all the time Joe has been gone. Now he has come home from his lark, broken in spirit and bankrupt in purse, and you are going to throw a big party! It's ridiculous...not fair."

The father can't understand why the elder

brother doesn't share his joy. *"Your brother was dead, and is alive again, was lost and is found!"* he explains, but I'm sure his words were not heard.

When we feel shortchanged, unappreciated or unloved, our reaction is invariably much the same as the steady-in-the-saddle brother. And like him, our envy spills over into self-pity and self-pity has such a narrow focus that it never leaves us enough room to celebrate another person's good fortune. We want equality, justice and fairness. And when life does not dispense what we think is our just due, we shout with the older brother, "We've been cheated and we're not gonna take it anymore. It's not fair!"

❦

For better or for worse, life does not keep books with the exactitude of an accountant. The "what you sow, you reap" principle applies to the *long* haul. Our recompense for kindness, generosity, caring, honesty and other virtues of the heart may not earn us dollar for dollar, hour for hour, stroke for stroke what we dispense. But it will in the long run produce some handsome dividends…tranquility that can be translated into sweet sleep, for instance. Like a stone tossed in a pond, the ripples that it creates can touch many an unseen shore.

❦

When I accept an invitation to speak, I usually share a little "art of living" philosophy of mine about the importance of paying compliments every day. In hopes of encouraging the practice, I stop mid-speech and ask those present to get up, mingle and exchange compliments with each other. The animated smiles and conversation that result from this little exercise confirms for me that praise is a commodity in short supply.

Some people eschew compliments, believing them to be full of soft soap, but that is only true if they contain "lye." There are two qualifications for all good compliments: They must be sincere and they must be specific. Generalities won't do.

"I liked your sermon" is three grades below, "I liked your explanation of David's prayer."

Or "I enjoyed your book," is inferior to "I found the chapter on pre-Columbian art fascinating."

Or "Thank you for the flowers," is less a winner than "How did you know that pink carnations were my favorite?"

I might add that I am extremely suspicious of the motives of one who forgoes compliments in favor of total honesty. They are often the same people who say such things as, "I'm only thinking of you," "This will hurt me more than it hurts you," and "I'm doing this for your own good." Spare me that truth.

The best advice I ever got on this subject is contained in this little maxim: *Love without honesty may be sentimentality, but honesty without love is brutality.*

It is obvious that when dealing with another's self esteem, we need great sensitivity and gentleness, carefully choosing words that are heartwarmers rather than heartchillers. Joyce Landorf, in her highly insightful book, *Irregular People,* tells the story of a woman who was an accomplished pianist who had played before large audiences around the country.

Once when conversation about her talent surfaced in the home of her parents, her father, who had never bothered to attend one of her concerts and had never complimented his daughter on her talent, volunteered: "You should hear Mrs. Brown play the piano...because she can *really* play."

Did the father hear his own words? Of course not. He was too busy talking to realize how they fell on his daughter's ears. He didn't know how much she longed for a word of praise from him. We need to do much more thinking before we speak and then more listening to our words to make sure they communicate exactly what we mean. What his daughter wanted to hear was the two sentences we all want to hear from our parents all our lives.

"I'm proud of you. I love you."

6

Finding Life's
Most Valuable Possession

❦

Like two lonely travelers
freezing in a storm,
Our hope is that together
we can keep each other warm.

Back in my newspaper reporting days, I was a feature writer, which meant that I covered everything from greased-pole climbs to rodeos, from soap-box derbies to Shirley Temple look-alike contests. Once I remember being sent out to a nursing home to do a piece on a woman who had lived to be one hundred years old. I suppose that I expected to find her half asleep in a rocking chair, but I got a big surprise.

Jenny not only greeted me enthusiastically at the door, she took my coat and hung it up. Then, she offered me tea that she had prepared herself. If eyes are the mirror of the soul, I thought, then, this woman has found Heaven. Still, it was her facile mind that impressed me most.

Naturally, I asked the stock reporter's question: "To what do you owe your longevity?" Her answer was anything but stock. "I'm very old by most standards, but," she said with a jaunty tilt of her head and a lifted eyebrow, "I'm frisky as a filly when it comes to mental age—the age that counts the most."

She went on to tell me how she spent her days, confined as she was to her room. Her activities included taking care of her plants, feeding and watching the birds that came to her window, listening to music, watching television news, reading the newspaper and good books ("I study my Bible 10 minutes every day"), telephoning friends and writing notes to "people who need to be encouraged," adding, "you know there are a lot of lonely and disheartened people in the world."

"Don't you get lonely all by yourself in a nursing home?" I asked.

"Do I get lonely? Sure everyone feels lonely from time to time, but my mother taught me when I was a child that there is a big difference between being lonely and being alone. Life's most valuable possession is peace of mind, and those who achieve it aren't bothered by silence. In fact, they thrive on it, for it is in quiet and solitude that we can best get in touch with ourselves."

❦

Getting in touch with ourselves. What Jenny

was really telling me but what, at the time, I was too young to comprehend, was that true contentment does not come from outside ourselves but from within. It doesn't come from other things or other people.

❧

And what about God? That depends on where you think God is. Jesus told the Pharisees that *"The Kingdom of God is within you."* I believe it. When God created us, He planted divine resources in us, seeds of His heaven, if you will. And He expects us to nurture those seeds until they become strong trees of hope, faith, trust and courage. It is when we draw on these God-given gifts that we draw near to Him.

Jenny's life was not easy. She had outlived her friends and some of her children. But she hadn't outlived her faith. Her peace of mind didn't come from material possessions, but spiritual ones. So will yours and mine.

❧

Before I became a newspaper feature writer and did stories on interesting people like Jenny, I wrote obituaries, an assignment for rookie reporters. So I spent a lot of time going through the "morgue," the place where biographical clippings on notable people were kept. Sometimes draft obituaries are written in advance of people's deaths as a way of having part of the article together ahead of time.

There is a story that is told about a famous man, one of the richest in his community, who one day visited a newspaper. The publisher gave him a tour of the plant. That included the "morgue." The businessman was amazed to learn that some obituaries are written before a person dies. He was even more surprised to learn that part of his already had been prepared. And when the publisher let his guest read what had been written about him, the visitor was even more amazed— and somewhat shocked. First of all, the obituary was very short. Secondly, it sounded very self-serving. On the basis of reading his own obituary, the businessman decided to change some ways. He reached out to touch his community. He gave of his time and money and concern to his community throughout his remaining years. His vision of himself and of his place in the scheme of life had been raised.

❧

We all need to have our vision raised. In days of old, ship captains taught young sailors how to adjust the sails of tall-masted schooners by sending

the trainees high above their ships right after

storms. Usually winds were still strong and the sea fierce, but the sky was clear and blue. Sometimes the inexperienced sailors would look down and, seeing the pitching sea, become so overcome with fear that they would freeze to the mast, unable to move.

"Don't look down," advice would come from below. "Look up." And when they did, the young sailors saw the stable sky and the steady horizon. It had a calming effect on them, and with their peace of mind restored, they were able to complete their tasks.

❧

You and I are rich beyond measure if we can look up. We are rich if we can feel God's nearness in storms as well as in the calm moments of life.

We are rich if we can know we were created in His image and imbued with His eternal gift of love.

We are rich when others turn to us for help, and we can touch them with encouragement.

We are rich when we are touched by others.

Someone sets love in motion. God begins the cycle but its sweet, healing music may never be heard, it's touch may never be felt if we do not pass it on. How? That is the touch of nearness.

❧

Just a touch of nearness—
a smile, a wave, a word
Can miracle a leafless tree
like a singing bird,
Just a touch of nearness—
a hug, a kiss, a note
Can re-ignite an inner light
and keep a soul afloat,
Just a touch of nearness
is all it sometimes takes
To catch a lost and lonely heart
before it falls and breaks.

Book design by Elizabeth Woll
Type set in Meridien